200+ frequently asked Interview Questions and Answers in Manual Testing

By Bandana Ojha

All Rights Reserved ©2018

Introduction

"200+ frequently asked Interview Questions and Answers in Manual Testing" book will help the reader to get a good understanding of manual testing methodology, concept, approaches and analysis. The author of this book conducted so many interviews at various companies and meticulously collected the most effective questions with simple, straightforward explanations. Rather than going through comprehensive, textbook-sized reference guides, this book includes only the information required to start his/her career as a manual tester. Answers of all the questions are short and to the point. We assure that you will get 90% frequently asked interview questions and answers going through this book. It is aimed at anyone who is interested to take a job in manual testing ranging from junior to expert level.

1. What is Quality Assurance?

Quality assurance is a process driven approach which checks that the process of developing the product is correct and meeting all user requirements. It involves activates like document review, test cases review, walkthroughs, inspection etc.

2. What is Quality Control?

Quality control is product driven approach which checks that the developed product conforms to all the specified requirements. It involves different types of testing like functional testing, performance testing, usability testing etc.

3. What is Software Testing?

Software testing is the process of evaluating a system to check if it satisfies its business requirements. It identifies the correctness, completeness and quality of the developed product.

4. Why is testing required?

We need software testing for following reasons-

1. Testing provides an assurance to the stakeholders that product works as intended.

2. Defects detected earlier phase of SDLC results into lesser cost and resource utilization of correction.

3. Saves development time by detecting issues in earlier phase of development.

4.Testing team adds another dimension to the software development by providing a different viewpoint to the product development process.

5.Avoidable defects leaked to the end user/customer without proper testing adds bad reputation to the development company.

5. What are the different levels of the testing?

Testing can be performed at different levels during the development process. Performing testing activities at multiple levels help in early identification of bugs. The different levels of testing are -

1.Unit Testing

2.Integration Testing

3.System Testing

4.Acceptance Testing

6. What is verification and validation?

Verification is a process of evaluating software at development phase and to decide whether the product of a given application satisfies the specified requirements.

Validation is the process of evaluating software at the end of the development process and to check whether it meets the customer requirements.

7. What is unit testing?

Unit testing is the first level of testing and it involves testing of individual modules of the software. It is usually performed by developers.

8. What is integration testing?

Integration testing is performed after unit testing. In integration testing we test the group of related modules. It aims at finding interfacing issues between the modules.

9. What are the different types of integration testing?

The different type of integration testing is,

1. Big bang Integration Testing - In big bang integration testing, testing starts only after all the modules are integrated.

2. Top-down Integration Testing - In top down integration, testing starts from top modules to lower level modules.

3. Bottom-up Integration Testing - In bottom up integration, testing starts from lower level modules to higher level module up in the hierarchy.

4. Hybrid Integration Testing - Hybrid integration testing is the combination of both Top-down and bottom up integration testing. In this approach, the integration starts from middle layer and testing is carried out in both the direction

10. What is system testing?

System testing is the level of testing where the complete software is tested. The conformance of the application with its business requirements is checked in system testing.

11. What is acceptance testing?

Acceptance testing is a testing performed by the potential end user or customers to check if the software conforms to the business requirements and can be accepted for use.

12. What is alpha testing?

Alpha testing is a type of acceptance testing that is performed end users at the developer site.

13. What is beta testing?

Beta testing is the testing done by end users at end user's site. It allows users to provide direct input about the software to the development company.

14. What is adhoc testing?

Adhoc testing is an unstructured way of testing that is performed without any formal documentation or proper planning.

15. What is monkey testing?

Monkey testing is a type of testing that is performed randomly without any predefined test cases or test inputs.

16. How is monkey testing different from adhoc testing?

In case of adhoc testing although there are no predefined or documented test cases still testers have, the understanding of the application. While in case of monkey testing testers doesn't have any understanding of the application.

17. What is risk-based testing?

Risk-based_testing is the term used for an approach to create a test strategy that is based on prioritizing tests by risk. The basis of the approach is a detailed risk analysis and prioritization of risks by risk level. Tests to address each risk are then specified, starting with the highest risk first.

18. What is the difference between black box and white box testing?

Black box testing is a type of testing in which internal architecture of the code is not required for testing. It is usually applicable for system and acceptance testing.

Whereas white box testing requires internal design and implementation knowledge of the application being tested. It is usually applicable for Unit and Integration testing.

19. What is the difference between smoke and sanity testing?

The difference between smoke and sanity testing is,

- Smoke testing is a type of testing in which the all major functionalities of the application are tested before carrying out exhaustive testing. Whereas sanity testing is subset of regression testing which is carried out when there is some minor fix in application in a new build.

- In smoke testing shallow-wide testing is carried out while in sanity narrow-deep testing (for a functionality) is done.

- The smoke tests are usually documented or are automated. Whereas the sanity tests are generally not documented or unscripted.

20. What is the difference between regression and retesting?

Regression testing is testing the application to verify that a new code change doesn't affect the other parts of the application. Whereas, in retesting we verify if the fixed issue is resolved or not.

21. What is mutation testing?

Mutation testing is a structural testing technique, which uses the structure of the code to guide the testing process. On a very high level, it is the process of rewriting the source code in small ways in order to remove the redundancies in the source code.

Mutation testing is a type of white box testing in which the source code of the application is mutated to cause some defect in its working. After that the test scripts are executed to check for their correctness by verifying the failures caused the mutant code.

22. What are the advantages of mutation testing?

Below are the advantages of mutation testing

It brings a whole new kind of errors to the developer's attention.

It is the most powerful method to detect hidden defects, which might be impossible to identify using the conventional testing techniques.

Increased customer satisfaction index as the product would be less buggy.

Debugging and Maintaining the product would be easier than ever.

23. What is decision testing or branch testing?

Decision testing or branch testing is a white box testing approach in which test coverage is measured by the percentage of decision points (e.g. if-else conditions) executed out of the total decision points in the application.

24. What is performance testing?

Performance testing is a type of non-functional testing in which the performance of the system is evaluated under expected or higher load. The various performance parameters evaluated during performance testing are - response time, reliability, resource usage, scalability etc.

25. What is load testing?

Load testing is a type of performance testing which aims at finding application's performance under expected workload. During load testing we evaluate the response time, throughput, error rate etc. parameters of the application.

26. What is stress testing?

Stress testing is a type of performance testing in which application's behavior is monitored under higher workload than expected. Stress testing is done to find memory leaks, robustness of the application as it is subjected to high workload.

27. What is volume testing?

Volume testing is a type of performance testing in which the performance of application is evaluated with large amount of data. It checks the scalability of the application and helps in identification of bottleneck with high volume of data.

28. What is concurrency testing?

Concurrency Testing is used to know the effects of using the software by different users at the same time. In this type of testing we have multiple users performing the exact same requests at the same time. It helps in identifying and measuring the problems in Response time, levels of locking and deadlocking in the application. For this we use Load runner to create VUGen (Virtual User Generator) is used to add the number of concurrent users and perform operation on the application on the same time.

29. What is endurance testing or Soak testing?

Endurance testing is a type of performance testing which aims at finding issues like memory leaks when an application is subjected to load test for a long period of time.

30. What is spike testing?

Spike testing is a type of load test. The object of this type of performance test is to verify a system's stability during bursts of concurrent user and or system activity to varying degrees of load over varying time periods.

31. What is usability testing?

Usability testing is the type of testing that aims at determining the extent to which the application is easy to understand and use.

32. What is Accessibility testing?

Accessibility is the type of testing which aims at determining the ease of use or operation of the application specifically by with disabilities.

33. What is Compatibility testing?

Testing software to see how compatible the software is with a environment - Operating system, platform or hardware.

34. What is configuration testing?

Configuration testing is the type of testing used to evaluate the configurational requirements of the software along with effect of changing the required configuration.

35. What is localization testing?

Localization testing is a type of testing in which we evaluate the application's customization (localized version of application) to a culture or locale. Generally, the content of the application is checked for updating (e.g. content language).

36. What is globalization testing?

Globalization testing is a type of testing in which application is evaluated for its functioning across the world.

37. What is negative testing?

Negative testing is a type of testing in which the application's robustness (graceful exiting or error reporting) is evaluated when provided with invalid input or test data.

38. What is security testing?

Security testing is a type of testing which aims at evaluating the integrity, authentication, authorization, availability, confidentiality and non-repudiation of the application under test.

39. What is penetration testing?

Penetration testing or pen testing is a type of security testing in which application is evaluated (safely exploited) for different kinds of vulnerabilities that any hacker could exploit.

40. What is robustness testing?

Robustness testing is a type of testing that is performed to find the robustness of the application i.e. the ability of the system to behave gracefully in case of erroneous test steps and test input.

41. What is A/B testing?

A/B testing is a type of testing in which the two variants of the software product are exposed to the end users and on analyzing the user behavior on each variant the better variant is chosen and used thereafter.

42. What is all pair testing?

All pair testing is a type of testing in which the application is tested with all possible combination of the values of input parameters.

43. What is dynamic testing?

Testing performed by executing or running the application under test either manually or using automation.

44. What is failover testing?

Failover testing is a type of testing that is used to verify application's ability to allocate more resources (more servers) in case of failure and transferring of the processing part to back-up system.

45. What is fuzz testing?

Fuzz testing is a type of testing in which large amount of random data is provided as input to the application to find security loopholes and other issues in the application.

46. What is UI testing?

UI or user interface testing is a type of testing that aims at finding Graphical User Interface defects in the application and checks that the GUI conforms to the specifications.

47. What is Model-Based testing?

Model-based testing is a software testing technique in which the test cases are derived from a model that describes the functional aspects of the system under test.

It makes use of a model to generate tests that includes both offline and online testing.

48. What is pilot testing?

Pilot testing is a testing carried out as a trial by limited number of users evaluate the system and provide their feedback before the complete deployment is carried out.

49. What is backend testing?

Backend testing is a type of testing that involves testing the backend of the system which comprises of testing the databases and the APIs in the application.

50. What is the difference between static and dynamic testing?

Static testing: During Static testing method, the code is not executed, and it is performed using the software documentation.

Dynamic testing: To perform this testing the code is required to be in an executable form.

51. What is random/monkey testing? When it is used?

Random testing often known as monkey testing. In such type of testing data is generated randomly often using a tool or automated mechanism. With this randomly generated input the system is tested, and results are analyzed accordingly. These testing are less reliable; hence it is normally used by the beginners and to see whether the system will hold up under adverse effects.

52. What is maintenance testing?

Maintenance Testing is done on the already deployed software. The deployed software needs to be enhanced, changed or migrated to other hardware. The Testing done during this enhancement, change and migration cycle is known as maintenance testing.

53. What is Boundary value testing?

Ans: Test boundary conditions on, below and above the edges of input and output equivalence classes. In boundary value testing we test only the exact boundaries, rather than hitting in the middle. That means we test above the maximum limit and below the minimum limit.

54. What is exploratory testing?

Exploratory testing is a hands-on approach in which testers are involved in minimum planning and maximum test execution. The planning involves the creation of a test charter, a short declaration of the scope of a short (1 to 2 hour) time-boxed test effort, the objectives and possible approaches to be used. The test design and test execution activities are performed in parallel typically without formally documenting the test conditions, test cases or test scripts. This does not mean that other, more formal testing techniques will not be used. For example, the tester may decide to use boundary value analysis but will think through and test the most important boundary values without necessarily writing them down. Some notes will be written during the exploratory-testing session, so that a report can be produced afterwards.

55. What is Equivalence partitioning testing?

Equivalence partitioning testing is a software testing technique which divides the application input test data into each partition at least once of equivalent data from which test cases can be derived. By this testing method it reduces the time required for software testing.

56. What is reliability testing?

Reliability testing is a testing strategy to measure the consistency of a Software in executing a specific operation without throwing any error for a certain period in the given environment.

57. What is Modularity Driven Testing?

Modularity driven testing is an automation testing framework in which small, independent modules of automation scripts are developed for the application under test. These individual scripts are constructed together to form a test realizing a particular test case.

58. What is benchmark testing?

Benchmarking testing is the process of comparing application performance with respect to industry standard which is given by some other organization. Benchmark informs us where our application stands with respect to others. Benchmark compares our application performance with other company's application's performance.

59. What is "use case testing"?

To identify and execute the functional requirement of an application from start to finish "use case" is used and the techniques used to do this is known as "Use Case Testing"

60. What is Agile testing and what is the importance of Agile testing?

Agile testing is software testing, is testing using Agile Methodology. The importance of this testing is that, unlike normal testing process, this testing does not wait for the development team to complete the coding first and then doing testing. The coding and testing both go simultaneously. It requires continuous customer interaction.

61. What is CRUD testing?

CRUD (Create, Read, Update and Delete) is another term used for Black box testing. CRUD testing is another term for database testing.

C – Create – Creating a new Transaction

R – Read/Retrieve – Searching or viewing a transaction

U – Update – Editing or modifying an existing transaction.

D – Delete – Deleting a transaction from the database

62. What is Workflow Testing?

Workflow processes technique in software testing by routing a record through each possible path. These tests are performed to ensure that each workflow process accurately reflects the business process. This kind of testing holds good for workflow-based applications.

63. What is N+1 testing?

The variation of regression testing is represented as N+1. In this technique the testing is performed in multiple cycles in which errors found in test cycle 'N' are resolved and re-tested in test cycle N+1. The cycle is repeated unless there are no errors found.

64. What is bottom up testing?

Bottom up testing is an approach to integration testing, where the lowest level components are tested first, then used to facilitate the testing of higher-level components. The process is repeated until the component at the top of the hierarchy is tested.

65. What is Baseline Testing?

A baseline is the indicator of a specific benchmark that serves as the foundation of a new creation.

In Baseline testing, the tests capture and preserve all the results produced by the source code and compare against a reference baseline. This reference baseline refers to the last accepted test results. If there are new changes in the source code, then it requires re-execution of tests to form the current baseline. If the new results get accepted, then the current baseline becomes the reference.

66. What is Cookie Testing?

Cookie Testing is the process of verifying whether the cookies are working as intended or not. In cookie testing, testers need to test the status of the cookie, expiration of cookie, accessibility of cookie, security constraints, etc.

67. What is the difference between Compatibility testing and Cross browser testing?

Compatibility testing: Testing an application on different hardware or software platform is Compatibility testing.

Example: Different devices such as iPhone, Samsung etc., Different operating system such as Windows, Linux etc.,

Cross browser testing: Testing a web application on different browsers is Cross browser testing. Cross browser testing is a subset of Compatibility testing.

Example: Google Chrome, IE 10, IE 11, Firefox etc.,

68. Which is a better testing methodology: black-box testing or white-box testing?

Both black-box and white-box testing approach have their own advantages and disadvantages. Black-box testing approach enables testers to externally test the system on the basis of specified requirement and specification and does not provide the scope of testing the internal structure of the system, whereas white-box testing methodology verify and validates the software quality through testing of its internal structure and working.

69. What is use case testing?

Ans. A use case testing is a black box testing approach in which testing is carried out using use cases. A use case scenario is seen as interaction between the application and actors(users). These use cases are used for depicting requirements and hence can also serve as basis for acceptance testing.

70. What is High Availability Testing?

High availability shows the ability of a system or a component to operate continuously without failure even at high loads for a long time.

Hence, the High availability testing confirms that a system or its sub-systems have gone through thorough checks and, in many cases, simulates failures to validate whether components support redundancy or not.

71. What is Storage Testing?

Testing that verifies the program under test stores data files in the correct directories and that it

reserves sufficient space to prevent unexpected termination resulting from lack of space. This is

external storage as opposed to internal storage.

72. What is rapid software testing?

Rapid software testing is a unique approach of testing which strikes out the need of any sort of documentation work and motivates testers to make use of their thinking ability and vision to carry out and drive the testing process.

73. What is Bucket Testing?

Bucket testing is a method to compare two versions of an application against each other to determine which one performs better.

74. What is SDLC?

Software Development Life Cycle refers to all the activities that are performed during software development, including - requirement analysis, designing, implementation, testing, deployment and maintenance phases.

75. What is STLC?

Software testing life cycle refers to all the activities performed during testing of a software product. The phases include-

1. Requirement analyses and validation - In this phase the requirements documents are analyzed and validated, and scope of testing is defined.

2. Test planning - In this phase test plan strategy is defined, estimation of test effort is defined along with automation strategy and tool selection is done.

3. Test Design and analysis - In this phase test cases are designed; test data is prepared, and automation scripts are implemented.

4. Test environment setup - A test environment closely simulating the real-world environment is prepared.

5. Test execution - The test cases are prepared, bugs are reported and retested once resolved.

6. Test closure and reporting - A test closure report is prepared having the final test results summary.

76. What is test cycle closure phase in STLC?

The testing team calls upon the meeting to evaluate the open defects, known issues, code quality issues and accordingly decides on the closure of the test cycle.

They discuss what went well, where is the need for improvement and notes the pain points faced in the current STLC. Such information is beneficial for the future STLC cycles. Each member puts his/her views on the test case & bug reports and finalizes the defect distribution by type and severity.

77. What is Rapid Application Development model (RAD)?

Rapid Application Development (RAD) is formally a parallel development of functions and subsequent integration. Components/functions are developed in parallel as if they were mini projects, the developments are time-boxed, delivered, and then assembled into a working prototype. This can very quickly give the customer something to see and use and to provide feedback regarding the delivery and their requirements. Rapid change and development of the product is possible using this methodology. However, the product specification will need to be developed for the product at some point, and the project will need to be placed under more formal controls prior to going into production.

78. Define a Test Case and a Use Case? What information would you include in their descriptions?

A test case is again a document which gives you a step by step detailed idea on how you can test an application. It usually comprises of results (pass or fail), remarks, steps, outputs, and description.

A use case on the other is a document of another kind. It helps you understand the actions of the user and the response of the system found in a particular functionality. It comprises of the cover page, revision, contents, exceptions, and pre and post conditions.

79. What is DRE?

To measure test effectiveness a powerful metric is used to measure test effectiveness known as DRE (Defect Removal Efficiency) From this metric we would know how many bugs we have found from the set of test cases. Formula for calculating DRE is

DRE=Number of bugs while testing / number of bugs while testing + number of bugs found by user

80. When do we prepare RTM (Requirement traceability matrix), is it before test case designing or after test case designing?

It would be before test case designing. Requirements should already be traceable from Review activities since you should have traceability in the Test Plan already. This question also would depend on the organization. If the organizations do test after development started, then requirements must be already traceable to their source. To make life simpler use a tool to manage requirements when the application is developed. Testing time is long, as we must test the whole application.

81. What is the difference between Desktop, Client server and Web testing?

Desktop application runs on personal computers and workstations, so when you test the desktop application you are focusing on a specific environment. You will test complete application broadly in categories like GUI, functionality, Load, and backend i.e. DB.

In client server application, you have two different components to test. Application is loaded on server machine while the application exe on every client machine. You will test broadly in categories like, GUI on both sides, functionality, Load, client-server interaction, backend. This environment is mostly used in Intranet networks. You are aware of number of clients and servers and their locations in the test scenario.

Web application is a bit different and complex to test as tester don't have that much control over the application. Application is loaded on the server whose location may or may not be known and no exe is installed on the client machine, you must test it on different web browsers. Web applications are supposed to be tested on different browsers and OS platforms so broadly Web application is tested mainly for browser compatibility and operating system compatibility, error handling, static pages, backend testing and load testing.

82. What is stub?

In case of Top-down integration many a times lower level modules are not developed while beginning testing/integration with top level modules. In those cases, Stubs or dummy modules are used that simulate the working of modules by providing hardcoded or expected output based on the input values.

83. What is driver?

In case of Bottom up integration drivers are used to simulate the working of top level modules to test the related modules lower in the hierarchy.

84. What is risk analysis?

Risk analysis is the analysis of the risk identified and assigning an appropriate risk level to it, based on its impact over the application.

85. What is a business requirements document (BRD)?

BRD provides a detailed business solution for a project including the documentation of customer needs and expectations.

BRD fulfills the following objectives.

Gain agreement with stakeholders.

Provide clarity on the business requirements.

Describe the solution that meets the customer/business needs.

Determine the input for the next phase of the project.

86. What is an exit criterion?

An exit criterion is a formal set of conditions that specify the agreed upon features or state of application to mark the completion of the process or product.

87. What are some advantages of automation testing?

Some advantages of automation testing are-

Test execution using automation is fast and saves considerable amount of time.

Carefully written test scripts remove the chance of human error during testing.

Tests execution can be scheduled for nightly run using CI tools like Jenkins which can also be configured to provide daily test results to relevant stakeholders.

Automation testing is very less resource intensive. Once the tests are automated, test execution requires almost no time of QAs. Saving QA bandwidth for other exploratory tasks.

88. What are some disadvantages of automation testing?

Some advantages of automation testing are-

1.It requires skilled automation testing experts to write test scripts.

2.Additional effort to write scripts is required upfront.

3.Automation scripts are limited to verification of the tests that are coded. These tests may miss some error that is very glaring and easily identifiable to human (manual QA).

4.Even with some minor change in application, script updating, and maintenance is required.

89. What is a test plan?

A test plan is a formal document describing the scope of testing, the approach to be used, resources required, and time estimate of carrying out the testing process. It is derived from the requirement documents (Software Requirement Specifications).

90. What is a test scenario?

A test scenario is derived from a use case. It is used for end to end testing of a feature of an application. A single test scenario can cater multiple test cases. The scenario testing is particularly useful when there is time constraint while testing.

91. What is a test case?

A test case is used to test the conformance of an application with its requirement specifications. It is a set of conditions with pre-requisites, input values and expected results in a documented form.

92. What is a test script?

A test script is an automated test case written in any programming or scripting language. These are basically a set of instructions to evaluate the functioning of an application.

93. What is a bug?

A bug is a fault in a software product detected at the time of testing, causing it to function in an unanticipated manner.

94. What is a defect?

A defect is non-conformance with the requirement of the product detected in production (after the product goes live).

95. What are some defect reporting attributes?

Some of the attributes of a Defect report are-

Defect Id - A unique identifier of the defect.

Defect Summary - A one-line summary of the defect, more like a defect title.

Defect Description - A detailed description of the defect.

Steps to reproduce - The steps to reproduce the defect.

Expected Result - The expected behavior from which the application is deviating because of the defect.

Actual Result- The current erroneous state of the application w.r.t. the defect.

Defect Severity - Based on the criticality of the defect, this field can be set to minor, medium, major or show stopper.

Priority - Based on the urgency of the defect, this field can be set on a scale of P0 to P3.

96. What are some of the bug or defect management tools?

Some of the most widely used Defect Management tools are - Jira, Bugzilla, Mantis, Quality Center etc.

97. What is defect priority?

A defect priority is the urgency of the fixing the defect. Normally the defect priority is set on a scale of P0 to P3 with P0 defect having the most urgency to fix.

98. What is defect severity?

Defect severity is the severity of the defect impacting the functionality. Based on the organization we can different levels of defect severity ranging from minor to critical or show stopper.

99. Give an example of Low Priority-Low severity, Low Priority-High severity, High Priority-Low severity, High Priority-High severity defects.

1. *Low Priority-Low severity* - A spelling mistake in a page not frequently navigated by users.

2. *Low Priority-High severity* - Application crashing in some very corner case.

3. *High Priority-Low severity* - Slight change in logo color or spelling mistake in company name.

4. *High Priority-High severity* - Issue with login functionality.

100. What is a blocker?

A blocker is a bug of high priority and high severity. It prevents or blocks testing of some other major portion of the application as well.

101. What is a critical bug?

A critical bug is a bug that impacts a major functionality of the application and the application cannot be delivered without fixing the bug. It is different from blocker bug as it doesn't affect or blocks the testing of other part of application.

102. What is the KEY difference between preventative and reactive approaches to testing?

Preventative tests are designed early; reactive tests are designed after the software has been produced.

103. What is the MAIN objective when reviewing a software deliverable?

To identify defects in any software work product.

104. As part of which test process do you determine the exit criteria?

The exit criteria are determined on the bases of 'Test Planning'.

105. What are the phases of a formal review?

In contrast to informal reviews, formal reviews follow a formal process. A typical formal review process consists of six main steps:

-Planning

-Kick-off

-Preparation

-Review meeting

-Rework

-Follow-up.

106. What is the MAIN benefit of designing tests early in the life cycle?

It helps prevent defects from being introduced into the code.

107. In white box testing what do you verify?

In white box testing following steps are verified.

1.Verify the security holes in the code

2.Verify the incomplete or broken paths in the code

3.Verify the flow of structure according to the document specification

4.Verify the expected outputs

5.Verify all conditional loops in the code to check the complete functionality of the application

6.Verify the line by line coding and cover 100% testing

108. When should testing be stopped?

It depends on the risks for the system being tested. There are some criteria bases on which you can stop testing.

-Deadlines (Testing, Release)

-Test budget has been depleted

-Bug rate fall below certain level

-Test cases completed with certain percentage passed

32

-Alpha or beta periods for testing ends

-Coverage of code, functionality or requirements are met to a specified point

109. Which of the following is the main purpose of the integration strategy for integration testing in the small?

The main purpose of the integration strategy is to specify which modules to combine when and how many at once.

110. What are the tables in test plans?

Test design, scope, test strategies, approach are various details that Test plan document consists of.

-Test case identifier

-Scope

-Features to be tested

-Features not to be tested

-Test strategy & Test approach

-Test deliverables

-Responsibilities

-Staffing and training

-Risk and Contingencies

111. What is traceability matrix?

The relationship between test cases and requirements is shown with the help of a document. This document is known as traceability matrix.

112. Mention the difference between Data Driven Testing and Retesting?

Retesting: It is a process of checking bugs that are actioned by development team to verify that they are fixed.

Data Driven Testing (DDT): In data driven testing process, application is tested with multiple test data. Application is tested with different set of values.

113. What are the valuable steps to resolve issues while testing?

Record: Log and handle any problems which has happened

Report: Report the issues to higher level manager

Control: Define the issue management process

114. What is the difference between test scenarios, test cases and test script?

Difference between test scenarios and test cases is that

Test Scenarios: Test scenario is prepared before the actual testing starts, it includes plans for testing product, number of team members, environmental condition, making test cases, making test plans and all the features that are to be tested for the product.

Test Cases: It is a document that contains the steps that must be executed, it has been planned earlier.

Test Script: It is written in a programming language and it's a short program used to test part of functionality of the software system. In other words, a written set of steps that should be performed manually.

115. What is Latent defect?

Latent defect: This defect is an existing defect in the system which does not cause any failure as the exact set of conditions has never been met

116. Why are static testing and dynamic testing described as complementary?

Because they share the aim of identifying defects but differ in the types of defect they find.

117. When is used Decision table testing?

Decision table testing is used for testing systems for which the specification takes the form of rules or cause-effect combinations. In a decision table, the inputs are listed in a column, with the outputs in the same column but below the inputs. The remainder of the table explores combinations of inputs to define the outputs produced.

118. Which of the following defines the expected results of a test? Test case specification or test design specification.

Test case specification defines the expected results of a test.

119. What is the benefit of test independence?

It avoids author bias in defining effective tests.

120. What is Process?

A process is a set of practices performed to achieve a given purpose; it may include tools, methods, materials or people.

121. What is a V-Model?

The V-Model is an extension of the waterfall model and is based on the association of a testing phase for each corresponding development stage. This means that for every single phase in the development cycle, there is a directly associated testing phase. This is a highly-disciplined model and the next phase starts only after completion of the previous phase.

122. What is test coverage?

Test coverage measures in some specific way the amount of testing performed by a set of tests (derived in some other way, e.g. using specification-based techniques). Wherever we can count things and can tell whether each of those things has been tested by some test, then we can measure coverage.

123. Why we split testing into distinct stages?

We split testing into distinct stages because of following reasons,

1. Each test stage has a different purpose

2. It is easier to manage testing in stages

3. We can run different test into different environments

4. Performance and quality of the testing is improved using phased testing

124. What are the two parameters which can be useful to know the quality of test execution?

To know the quality of test execution we can use two parameters

-Defect reject ratio

-Defect leakage ratio

125. What all things you should consider before selecting automation tools for the AUT?

-Technical Feasibility

-Complexity level

-Application stability

-Test data

-Application size

-Re-usability of automated scripts

-Execution across environment

126. Why is incremental integration preferred over "big bang" integration?

Ans: Because incremental integration has better early defects screening and isolation ability

127. What is the purpose of a test completion criterion?

Ans: The purpose of test completion criterion is to determine when to stop testing

128. What is your approach when requirements change continuously?

-Write generic test plans and test cases which focus on the intent of the requirement rather than its exact details

-Work very closely with the product owners or business analysts to understand the scope of change so testing can be updated

-Make sure the team understands the risks involved in changing requirements especially towards the end of sprint

-If you're going to automate this feature, it is best to wait until the feature is stable and requirements are finalized

-Negotiate to see if the changes can be kept to a minimum and/or implement the changes in next sprint

129. What are the two key factors when working as a QA in an Agile team?

Ans: QA can add a lot of value to an agile team because of the different mindset. Testers can and should think about the different possible scenarios to test a story. However, the most important asset that they can bring is:

-To prevent defect. QA should advocate best practices along the way to prevent defects from entering the system in the first place.

-To provide fast feedback. It is important for developers to know if the new functionality works as expected and if regression tests pass, and they need that feedback quite quickly. QA should provide the results of the tests to developers as soon as possible.

130. What is showstopper defect?

A defect which is not permitting to continue further with testing is called Showstopper Defect.

131. What is the purpose of test design technique?

Identifying test conditions and Identifying test cases.

132. Explain bug lifecycle?

A bug goes through the following phases in software development-

New - A bug or defect when detected is in New state

Assigned - The newly detected bug when assigned to the corresponding developer is in Assigned state

Open - When the developer works on the bug, the bug lies in Open state

Rejected/Not a bug - A bug lies in rejected state in case the developer feels the bug is not genuine

Deferred - A deferred bug is one, fix of which is deferred for some time (for the next releases) based on urgency and criticality of the bug

Fixed - When a bug is resolved by the developer it is marked as fixed

Test - When fixed the bug is assigned to the tester and during this time the bug is marked as in Test

Reopened - If the tester is not satisfied with issue resolution the bug is moved to Reopened state

Verified - After the Test phase if the tester feels bug is resolved, it is marked as verified

Closed - After the bug is verified, it is moved to Closed status.

133. What is the role of moderator in review process?

The moderator (or review leader) leads the review process. He or she determines, in co-operation with the author, the type of review, approach and the composition of the review team. The moderator performs the entry check and the follow-up on the rework, to control the quality of the input and output of the review process. The moderator also schedules the meeting, disseminates documents before the meeting, coaches other team members, paces the meeting, leads possible discussions and stores the data that is collected.

134. What is defect density?

Defect density is the measure of density of the defects in the system. It can be calculated by dividing number of defect identified by the total number of line of code (or methods or classes) in the application or program.

135. What is Testware?

Testware is test artifacts like test cases, test data, test plans needed to design and execute a test.

136. What is the difference between build and release?

Build: It is a number given to Installable software that is given to the testing team by the development team.

Release: It is a number given to Installable software that is handed over to the customer by the tester or developer.

137. What is bug leakage and bug release?

Bug release is when software or an application is handed over to the testing team knowing that the defect is present in a release. During this the priority and severity of bug is low, as bug can be removed before the final handover.

Bug leakage is something, when the bug is discovered by the end users or customer, and not detected by the testing team while testing the software

138. What is quality audit?

The systematic and independent examination for determining the effectiveness of quality control procedures is known as the quality audit.

139. What is a 'USE' case and what does it include?

The document that describes, the user action and system response, for a particular functionality is known as USE case. It includes revision history, table of contents, flow of events, cover page, special requirements, pre-conditions and post-conditions.

140. What is silk test and why should you use it?

Here are some facts about the Silk tool.

1. It's a tool developed for performing the regression and functionality testing of the application.

2. It benefits when we are testing Window based, Java, the web, and the traditional client/server applications.

3. Silk Test help in preparing the test plan and managing them to provide the direct accessing of the database and validation of the field.

141. How do you plan test automation?

1) Prepare the automation Test plan 2) Identify the scenario 3) Record the scenario 4) Enhance the

scripts by inserting check points and Conditional Loops 5) Incorporated Error Handler 6) Debug the

script 7) Fix the issue 8) Rerun the script and report the result.

142. Can test automation improve test effectiveness?

Yes, automating a test makes the test process: 1) Fast 2) Reliable 3) Repeatable 4) Programmable 5)

Reusable 6) Comprehensive

143. What are the main attributes of test automation?

software test automation attributes : Maintainability - the effort needed to update the test automation

suites for each new release Reliability - the accuracy and repeatability of the test automation

Flexibility - the ease of working with all the different kinds of automation test ware Efficiency - the total

cost related to the effort needed for the automation Portability - the ability of the automated test to run

on different environments Robustness - the effectiveness of automation on an unstable or rapidly

changing system Usability - the extent to which automation can be used by different types of users

144. Does automation replace manual testing?

There can be some functionality which cannot be tested in an automated tool so we may have to do it

manually. Therefore, manual testing can never be replaced. (We can write the scripts for negative

testing also but it is hectic task).When we talk about real environment we do negative testing

manually.

43

145. What is a cause effect graph?

Ans. A cause effect graph testing is black box test design technique in which graphical representation of input i.e. cause and output i.e. effect is used for test designing. This technique uses different notations representing AND, OR, NOT etc relations between the input conditions leading to output.

146. What is Intranet Application?

Intranet application is a kind of private application which is deployed and run on local LAN server and can only be accessed by the people within the organization. It uses local network to share information.

147. What are the Experience-based testing techniques?

In experience-based techniques, people's knowledge, skills and background are a prime contributor to the test conditions and test cases. The experience of both technical and business people is important, as they bring different perspectives to the test analysis and design process. Due to previous experience with similar systems, they may have insights into what could go wrong, which is very useful for testing.

148. What is Fault Masking?

Error condition hiding another error condition is called fault masking.

149. How is testing affected by object-oriented designs?

Well-engineered object-oriented design can make it easier to trace from code to internal design to

functional design to requirements. While there will be little affect on black box testing (where an

understanding of the internal design of the application is unnecessary), white-box testing can be

oriented to the application's objects. If the application was well-designed this can simplify test design.

150. What is Extreme Programming ?

Extreme Programming (XP) is a software development approach for small teams on risk-prone

projects with unstable requirements. It was created by Kent Beck who described the approach in his

book 'Extreme Programming Explained'.

151. What is EP got to do with testing?

Testing is a core aspect of Extreme Programming. Programmers are expected to write unit and functional test code first - before the application is developed. Test code is under source control along with the rest of the code. Customers are expected to be an integral part of the project team and to help develop scenarios for acceptance/black box testing. Acceptance tests are preferably automated and are modified and rerun for each of the frequent development iterations. QA and test personnel are also required to be an integral part of the project team. Detailed requirements documentation is not

45

used, and frequent re-scheduling, re-estimating, and re-prioritizing is expected.

152. How you will describe testing activities?

Testing activities start from the elaboration phase. The various testing activities are preparing the test

plan, preparing test cases, Execute the test case, Log the bug, validate the bug & take appropriate

action for the bug, Automate the test cases.

153. What are error guessing and error seeding?

Error Guessing.

It is a test case design technique in which testers have to guess the defects that might occur and write test cases to represent them.

Error Seeding.

It is the process of adding known bugs in a program for the tracking the rate of detection & removal. It also helps to estimate the number of faults remaining in the program.

154. How is a test case different from a test scenario?

A test case is a testing artifact to verify a particular flow with defined input values, test preconditions, expected output, and postconditions prepared to cover specific behavior.

A test scenario can have one or many associations with a test case which means it can include multiple test cases.

155. What is defect clustering?

Defect clustering is a situation in testing which could arise if either most of the software bugs got discovered only in a handful of modules or the software fails to operate frequently.

156. What is pesticide paradox?

The pesticide paradox is a situation in software testing when the same tests get repeated over and over again until they are no longer able to find new bugs.

157. What is the pareto principle?

In software testing, the Pareto Principle refers to the notion that 80% of all bugs happen to be in the 20% of the program modules.

158. What is the difference between coupling and cohesion?

The difference between coupling and cohesion is as follows.

Cohesion is the degree which measures the dependency of the software component that combines related functionality into a single unit whereas coupling represents to have it in a different group.

Cohesion deals with the functionality that relates to different processes within a single module whereas coupling deals with how much one module is dependent on the other modules within the product.

It is a good practice to increase the cohesion between the software whereas coupling is discouraged.

159. What is cyclomatic complexity in software testing?

In software testing, the cyclomatic complexity represents a test metric known as the program complexity. This method got introduced by Thomas J. McCabe in the year 1976. It sees a program as a graph using the control flow representation.

The graph includes the following attributes:

1. Nodes – A node indicates the processing tasks

2. Edges – An edge shows the control flow between the nodes.

160. What is CAST?

Computer Aided Software Testing refers to the computing-based processes, techniques and tools for

testing software applications or programs.

161. What is Cause Effect Graph?

A graphical representation of inputs and the associated outputs effects which can be used to design

test cases.

162. What is Code Complete?

Phase of development where functionality is implemented entirety; bug fixes are all that are left. All

functions found in the Functional Specifications have been implemented.

163. What is Code Coverage?

An analysis method that determines which parts of the software have been executed (covered) by the

test case suite and which parts have not been executed and therefore may require additional

attention.

164. What is Code Inspection?

A formal testing technique where the programmer reviews source code with a group who ask

questions analyzing the program logic, analyzing the code with respect to a checklist of historically

common programming errors and analyzing its compliance with coding standards. Know more about

the Inspection in software testing.

165. What is Code Walkthrough?

A formal testing technique where source code is traced by a group with a small set of test cases,

while the state of program variables is manually monitored, to analyze the programmer's logic and assumptions. Know more about Walkthrough in software testing.

166. What is Data Dictionary?

A database that contains definitions of all data items defined during analysis.

167. What is scrum?

A scrum is a process for implementing Agile methodology. In scrum, time is divided into sprints and on completion of sprints, a deliverable is shipped.

168. What is the difference between testing and debugging?

Testing is the primarily performed by testing team in order to find the defects in the system. Whereas, debugging is an activity performed by development team. In debugging the cause of defect is located and fixed. Thus, removing the defect and preventing any future occurrence of the defect as well.

Other difference between the two is - testing can be done without any internal knowledge of software architecture. Whereas debugging requires knowledge of the software architecture and coding.

169. Explain equivalence class partitioning.

Equivalence class partitioning is a specification based black box testing techniques. In equivalence class partitioning, set of input data that defines different test conditions are partitioned into logically similar groups such that using even a single test data from the group for testing can be considered as similar to using all the other data in that group. E.g. for testing a Square program(program that prints the square of a number- the equivalence classes can be-

Set of Negative numbers, whole numbers, decimal numbers, set of large numbers etc.

170. What is Race Condition?

A race condition is an undesirable situation that occurs when a device or system attempts to perform

two or more operations at the same time, but because of the nature of the device or system, the

operations must be done in the proper sequence to be done correctly.

171. What is Testability?

The degree to which a system or component facilitates the establishment of test criteria and the

performance of tests to determine whether those criteria have been met.

172. What are memory leaks and buffer overflows?

Memory leak:

A bug in a program that prevents it from freeing up memory that it no longer needs. As a result, the program grabs more and more memory until it finally crashes because there is no more memory left.

Buffer overflow :

Buffer overflow occurs when a program or process tries to store more data in a buffer (temporary data storage area) than it was intended to hold. Since buffers are created to contain a finite amount of data, the extra information - which has to go somewhere - can overflow into adjacent buffers, corrupting or overwriting the valid data held in them.

173. What is test suite?

A test suite is a collection of test cases that are intended to be used to test a software program to show that it has some specified set of behaviors. A test suite often contains detailed instructions or goals for each collection of test cases and information on the system configuration to be used during testing. A group of test cases may also contain prerequisite states or steps, and descriptions of the following tests.

174. What is Dynamic analysis tools in software testing?

Dynamic analysis tools are 'dynamic' because they require the code to be in a running state. They are 'analysis' rather than 'testing' tools because they analyze what is happening 'behind the scenes' that is in the code while the software is running (whether being executed with test cases or being used in operation).

175. What are incident reports in software testing?

After logging the incidents that occur in the field or after deployment of the system we also need some way of reporting, tracking, and managing them. It is most common to find defects reported against the code or the system itself. However, there are cases where defects are reported against requirements and design specifications, user and operator guide and tests also.

176. What is Incident management tools?

Incident management tool is also known as a defect-tracking tool, a defect-management tool, a bug-tracking tool or a bug-management tool. However, 'incident management tool' is perhaps a better name for it because not all of the things tracked are actually defects or bugs; incidents may also be perceived problems, anomalies that are not necessarily be defects. Also, what is normally recorded is information about the failure (not the defect) that was generated at the time of testing and the information about the defect that caused that failure would come to light when someone (e.g. a developer) begins to look into the failure.

177. What is the difference between a test driver and test stub?

The test driver is a piece of code that calls a software component under test. It is useful in testing that follows the bottom-up approach.

Test stub is a dummy program that integrates with an application to complete its functionality. These are relevant for testing that uses the top-down approach.

178. How do you test a product if the requirements are yet to freeze?

If the requirement spec is not available for a product, then a test plan can be created based on the assumptions made about the product. But we should get all assumptions well documented in the test plan.

179. What are the entry and exit criteria in software testing?

Entry criteria – It is a process that should run when a system begins. It includes the following artifacts.

SRS (Software Requirement Specification)

FRS (Functional Requirement Specification)

Use case

Test-Case

Test-plan

Exit Criteria – It signals when the testing should complete and when should the product be ready to release. It includes the following artifacts.

Test Summary Report

Metrics

Defect Analysis report

180. What is pesticide paradox?

The pesticide paradox is a situation in software testing when the same tests get repeated over and over again until they are no longer able to find new bugs.

181. What is the purpose of a failover test?

Failover testing is a test strategy to evaluate how a software allocates resources and switch operations to backup systems for preventing operational failures.

182. How to deal with not reproducible bug?

A bug cannot be reproduced for following reasons:

1. Low memory.

2. Addressing to non-available memory location.

3. Things happening in a particular sequence.

Tester can do following things to deal with not reproducible bug:

- Includes steps that are close to the error statement.

- Evaluate the test environment.

- Examine and evaluate test execution results.

- Resources & Time Constraints must be kept in point.

183. What is concurrent user hits in load testing?

When the multiple users, without any time difference, hits on a same event of the application under the load test is called a concurrent user hit. The concurrency point is added so that multiple Virtual User can work on a single event of the application. By adding concurrency point, the virtual users will wait for the other Virtual users which are running the scripts, if they reach early. When all the users reached to the concurrency point, only then they start hitting the requests.

184. Explain Branch Coverage and Decision Coverage.

- Branch Coverage is testing performed in order to ensure that every branch of the software is executed at least once. To perform the Branch coverage testing we take the help of the Control Flow Graph.

- Decision coverage testing ensures that every decision taking statement is executed at least once.

- Both decision and branch coverage testing is done to ensure the tester that no branch and decision taking statement, will not lead to failure of the software.

176. What is Statement coverage?

Statement Coverage is a metric used in White Box Testing. Statement coverage is used to ensure that all the statement in the program code is executed at least once. The advantages of Statement Coverage are:

- Verifies that written code is correct.

- Measures the quality of code written.

- Determine the control flow of the program.

- To Calculate Statement Coverage:

- Statement Coverage = Statements Tested / Total No. of Statements.

177. What should be done after a bug is found?

After finding the bug the first step is bug to be locked in bug report. Then this bug needs to be communicated and assigned to developers that can fix it. After the bug is fixes by the developer, fixes should be re-tested, and determinations made regarding requirements for regression testing to check that fixes didn't create problems elsewhere.

178. What if the software is so buggy it can't really be tested at all?

In this situation is for the testers to go through the process of reporting of bugs with the focus being on critical bugs. Since this type of problem can severely affect schedules and indicates deeper problems in the software development process project managers should be notified and provided with some documentation.

179. What are the advantages of waterfall model?

The advantages of the waterfall model are:

- Simple to implement and required fewer amounts of resources.

- After every phase output is generate.

- Help in methods of analysis, design, coding, testing and maintenance.

- Preferred in projects where quality is more important than schedule and cost.

- Systematic and sequential model.

- Proper documentation of the project.

180. What is gap analysis?

Gap analysis reveals any deviation between the features available for testing and how the customer perceives them to be.

Traceability matrix is a testing tool which testers can use to track down the gaps.

181. What are the test artifacts involved in QA?

The test artifacts involved in QA are Test Strategy, Test Plan, Test Scenarios, Test Cases, Test Summary Report, Bug Report etc.

182. What is Bug triage?

Bug triage is a formal process to find which bugs are important by prioritizing them based on their severity, frequency, risk and other important parameters. Testers assign priority (high, medium, low) to each and every bug in a bug triage meeting and based on the priority those bugs will be fixed in an order.

183. What is MR and ER?

MR: MR stands for Modification Request. It is used to change the existing functionality in a software, it is usually requested by clients.

ER: ER stands for Enhancement report. It is used to add a new feature in a software. It is usually requested by clients.

184. What is a Cookie?

A Cookie is a small piece of information sent from a website and stored on the users in the users hard drive (in a text file) by the user's web browser while the user is browsing and is sent back to the website each time the browser requests a page from the website. Cookies were designed to track the users browsing activities such as login credentials, visited pages or to store stateful information such as items added in the shopping cart in an online store or to record the information which was filled by the user in the form fields such as name, card details, address details etc.

185. When, what and why to automate?

Automation is preferred when the execution of tests needs to be carried out repetitively for a longer period of time and within the specified deadlines. Further, an analysis of ROI on automation is desired to analyses the cost-benefit model of the automation. Preferably functional, regression and functional tests may be automated. Further, tests which requires accuracy and precision, and is time-consuming may be considered for automation, including data driven tests also.

186. Are test coverage and code coverage similar terms?

No, code coverage amounts the percentage of code covered during software execution whereas test coverage concerns with the test cases to cover specified functionality and requirement.

187. What is Test Bed?

Test bed is an environment configured for testing. Test bed consists of hardware, software, network configuration, an application under test, other related software.

188. What is big bang approach?

Big bang approach is ,combining all the modules once and verifying the functionality after completion of individual module testing.

Top down and bottom up are carried out by using dummy modules known as Stubs and Drivers. These Stubs and Drivers are used to stand-in for missing components to simulate data communication between modules.

189. What is a test harness? Why do we need a test harness?

A test harness is a collection of test scripts and test data usually associated with unit and integration testing. It involves stubs and drivers that are required for testing software modules and integrated components.

190. What is HotFix?

 HotFix is a bug which needs to handle as a high priority bug and fix it immediately.

191. What is the importance of database testing?

Database is an inherited component of a software application as it works as a backend system of the application and stores different types of data and information from multiple sources. Thus, it is crucial to test the database to ensure integrity, validity, accuracy and security of the stored data.

192. What are the steps involved in structured testing?

Below are the steps:

The control flow graph should get derived from the system component.

The Cyclomatic Complexity of the chart should get considered.

A group of C basis path should get identified.

Defining test cases for every basis path is necessary.

The execution should include all the established test cases.

193. What is age of defect in software testing?

Defect age is the time elapsed between the day the tester discovered it and the day the developer got this fixed.

While estimating the age of a defect, consider the following points.

1. The day of birth for a Defect is the day it got assigned and accepted by the dev.

2. The issues which got dropped are out of the scope.

3. The age can be both in hours or days.

4. The end time is the day got verified and closed, not just fixed by the dev.

194. What is the difference between baseline and benchmark testing?

Baseline testing runs a set of tests to determine the performance and Benchmark testing compares the application performance with industry standards. Baseline testing strives to improve performance with the help of collected information, on the other hand, benchmark testing seeks to improve application performance by matching it with benchmarks.

195. What are the points that are covered while planning phase of automation?

During planning phase of automation things which must be taken in concern are

Selection the "right" Automation tool

Selection Automation Framework if any

List of in scope and out of scope items for automation

Test Environment Setup

Preparing Grant Chart of Project timelines for test script development & execution.

Identify Test Deliverables

196. How Agile Testing is different to the traditional waterfall or the V model?

The big difference is that in an agile environment, testing is not a phase, it is an activity parallel to development.

In an agile environment, small features of the software are delivered frequently, so testing activity should be parallel to development activity. Testing time is short as we are only testing small features.

In the waterfall model, there is a testing phase at the end of the development so, testing is a big effort done after the whole application is developed. Testing time is long as we have to test the whole application.

197. What are the two key factors when working as a QA in an Agile team?

QAs can add a lot of value to an agile team because of the different mindset. Testers can and should think about the different possible scenarios to test a story. However, the most important asset that they can bring is:

To prevent defect. QA should advocate best practices along the way to prevent defects from entering the system in the first place.

To provide fast feedback. It is important for developers to know if the new functionality works as expected and if regression tests pass, and they need that feedback quite quickly. QA should provide the results of the tests to developers as soon as possible.

198. What are the three main roles in Scrum?

The Scrum team consists of three main roles:

Product Owner: Manages the product backlog. PO is the voice of the business and creates new features to be developed for the application.

Scrum Master: Responsible for managing the sprint, remove any impediments and keeps track of the progress of the project.

Scrum Team itself: Composed of developers, designers, and QA. This forms the team which is responsible for delivering high-quality software.

199. How is Web Application Testing different to Desktop Application Testing?

Web Applications are typically hosted on a server which we can access via a web browser, whereas desktop applications are installed on the client's machine.

This setup opens a lot of new testing challenges: Performance and Security testing become important as the application is open to a wide audience. Good design and usability are also important.

Other important factors that come to play are testing on multiple browsers, multiple devices, redirection, and responsiveness.

Also, we should not forget about JavaScript, CSS, Cookies, W3C standards, traffic monitoring, third-party tags testing, all of which are important in Web Application Testing.

200. What is a Sprint?

In Scrum, the project is divided into Sprints. Each Sprint has a specified timeline (2 weeks to 1 month). This timeline will be agreed by a Scrum Team during the Sprint Planning Meeting. Here, User Stories are split into different modules. The end result of every Sprint should be a potentially shippable product.

201. What is product backlog?

Product Backlog is a repository where the list of Product Backlog Items stored and maintained by the Product Owner. The list of Product Backlog Items are prioritized by the Product Owner as high and low and also could re-prioritize the product backlog constantly.

202. What is sprint backlog?

Group of user stories which scrum development team agreed to do during the current sprint (Committed Product Backlog items). It is a subset of the product backlog.

203. What is the difference between Burn-up and Burn-down chart?

Burn-up charts represent how much work has been completed in a project whereas Burn-down chart represents the remaining work left in a project.

Burn Down Charts provide proof that the project is on track or not. Both burn-up and burn-down charts are graphs used to track the progress of a project.

Please check this out:

Our other best-selling books are-

500+ Java & J2EE Interview Questions & Answers- Java & J2EE Programming

200+ Frequently Asked Interview Questions & Answers in iOS Development

200 + Frequently Asked Interview Q & A in SQL , PL/SQL, Database Development & Administration

100+ Frequently Asked Interview Questions & Answers in Scala

100+ Frequently Asked Interview Q & A in Swift Programming

100+ Frequently Asked Interview Q & A in Python Programming

100+ Frequently Asked Interview Questions & Answers in Android Development

Frequently asked Interview Q & A in Java programming

Frequently Asked Interview Questions & Answers in J2EE

Frequently asked Interview Q & A in Mobile Testing

Frequently asked Interview Q & A in Test Automation- Selenium Testing

www.ingramcontent.com/pod-product-compliance
Lightning Source LLC
Chambersburg PA
CBHW030502220526
45464CB00006B/2620